*Who is going to believe
they saved or prolonged...*

MY LIFE

*Who is going to believe
they saved or prolonged...*

MY LIFE

CARL KEGERREIS

Copyright © 2022 by Carl Kegerreis. All rights reserved.

No part of this book may be reproduced or transmitted in any form or by any means, electronic or mechanical, including photocopying, recording, or by any information storage and retrieval system, without written permission of the publisher.

ISBN Paperback: 978-1-77419-167-5

ISBN eBook: 978-1-77419-168-2

To order additional copies of this book, please contact:

eComRocket, LLC www.ecomrocket.net

3rd Floor 4915 54 St Red Deer, Alberta T4N 2G7 Canada

General Inquiries & Customer Service:

Phone: 1-(403)-755-8677

Toll Free: 1-(866)-269-9719

Email: info@ecomrocket.net

Book cover copyright © 2022 by eComRocket, LLC. All rights reserved.

Published in Canada

ACKNOWLEDGMENTS

A special thank you to all the employees, the staff, the nurses, the doctors, and the administrators at the Cleveland, Ohio, Clinic.

Special thanks to the clinic's Legal Department; Amanda Hollis, director of the clinic's Department of Development; and Eileen_ Sheil, director of the clinic's Communications Department, who have reviewed my manuscript, author izing this manuscript to be published.

Thanks to my wife, Sandra, who stayed with me at the clinic: our son, Robert, and my brother Bob, who helped us travel from our home to the clinic and return to our home; and our daughter Carla and her husband, Michael, who surprised us by paying our first motel bill and handling the arrangements for us to stay at the Hilton Homewood Suites before my surgery at the clinic.

Thanks to all our family and friends who prayed for my recovery.

Special thanks to Dr. Michael Applebaum, who has been our family doctor for twenty-three years, who found the swelling in my abdomen during my physical, requiring me to get a CT scan and to see a Toledo surgeon who suggested that I go to a cancer center. I chose the Cleveland Clinic, which I give credit to for saving or prolonging my life.

CONTENTS

Foreword vii
Our Daughter's Poems 1
   I Was Afraid 1
   God 2
   The Disease 3
   The Fight 4
   In Control 5
   The Game 5
   I Have Spoken 7
   The Voice 8
   Dear God 8
   My Disease 9
Surprise 11
More Surprises 19
Thank You, God, for Doctors, Nurses, and the Cleveland Clinic 27
Did We Get the Little Devil? 42
The Little Devil's Friend 52
Additional Information 62
About the Author 63

FOREWORD

All royalty proceeds from this book will be donated to the Cleveland Clinic Foundation at PO Box 931517, Cleveland, Ohio, 44101-8713. The donations by check will be made payable to the Cleveland clinic for cancer research. I was in such a place at the Cleveland Clinic in Cleveland, Ohio, I could not begin to tell you how I was nervous, upset, and how I attempted to appear acting normal in front of my wife, Sandra, and our son, Rob, who were with me on September 22, 2011. I give credit to a Baptist chaplain, Charissa Prunty, a God-loving woman who was with me in the preparation room prior to going upstairs for surgery. She held my hand and prayed with me and my family. Now, please don't get the idea I was on my deathbed, although there was that possibility. I have to tell you after the prayer I was on my way upstairs, and I felt so much calmer, with a warm feeling from the tip of my toes to the top of my head. I was lying on a stretcher as the hospital staff rolled me into a room that reminded me of a warehouse but had partitions and curtains. I sat up as required. I felt a pinch on my back with someone telling me, "You are going to feel pain as we push the needle in your spine, but it will help control your surgery pain. Does it hurt?" I nodded my head no and was asked to lie down. I believe that the chaplain's prayer and that warm feeling in me helped my pain. Also, I knew that our family and friends were praying for me. I shall be for ever grateful for their prayers. I was brought into this world by a wonderful mother and a father who was a Protestant Methodist minister.

Now I ask you, do you believe in guardian angels? I will tell you why I believe. I was seven when I decided to leave our yard and run across a *busy highway*, not looking each way for any vehicle traveling on *Indiana State Route* 15. You guessed it. The car was on me, so I jumped up on the front bumper and grabbed the hood ornament. Sorry to say, the driver hit the brakes, and the concrete greeted me. I ended up in the local doctor's office, getting my head bandaged. I remember seeing my parents, the town under taker, a church member, my brother, but I never did see the person driving the car. I believe my guardian angel held me on the car bumper and softened my blow when falling to the concrete road. Several years later, my brother and I were playing tag in the Methodist parsonage upstairs when I slid and fell through the window, breaking the glass, and was suddenly stopped from falling about twenty-five feet to the ground. My brother had raced down the stairs while I was sliding down the hallway, so someone-my *guardan angel-grabbed* me and kept me from falling out the window. I wished that my guardian angel had stopped Dad from spanking me.

Years later, we had moved to another city, and I will never forget my older brother, Marvin, who was mad at me. He acted like he was going to hit me with a baseball, and I backed through the front picture window on the front porch of the Methodist parsonage. I ended up in the front room with broken glass everywhere and on me, but I'm not hurt, though I can't say the same for my rear end. Once again, my guardian angel failed to protect me from my angry father.

I was a police captain working on the CSX Transportation Railroad in Pittsburgh, Pennsylvania, when I was contacted on my railroad police radio by our train crew to check for kids releasing the hand brakes on the couplers of their coal train. I gave the crew instructions-"Do not move the train until I tell you it's okay." I crossed over in between two coal cars looking for kids, walking on a car coupler, start ing to jump down on the rails, when someone grabbed me, pulling me backward and causing me to fall from the car coupler. Falling to the ground, I was amazed as I watched a Pittsburgh passenger train roll by where I would have been standing. I thanked God and my guardian angel.

So yes, I believe in guardian angels, and I believe my angel was with me and talked to me (which will be explained later) while I remained in the Cleveland Clinic. I had asked myself; *Do I really need to go to the clinic? What could I have done different?*

I am here today, writing this book, satisfied knowing that *this information will help any person who discovers that they have a disease like mine. I want the reader to understand why a yearly physical is so important, and that there is a great hospital for treatment of this disease, which is the Cleveland Clinic.*

Please look once again at the front cover of this book; Illustrating an angel with God's Love," which explains the Cleveland Clinic. I have never been at a hospital where there was so much concern for myself and my wife, Sandra, who stayed with me. The love, trust, and friendship were overwhelming. I have been in other hospitals as a child and as an adult where I wanted to leave. I have to admit it was great news after two weeks when my doctor told me I could return home. Sandra and I will never forget the Clinic's friendship.

Please note that the retroperitoneal mass-a malignant tumor-which I will refer to as the Litt le Devil was removed from my abdomen during my surgery at the Cleveland Clinic. The tumor removed was round and the size of a soccer ball.

OUR DAUGHTER'S POEMS

Our daughter Robin, the mother of two daughters, entered God's kingdom on November 15, 1999. She bravely fought but lost the battle with cervix cancer at age twenty-eight. During her battle and struggle with her cancer, Robin wrote several poems that our family wants to share with you.

(A Collection of My Poems, copyright © 1999 by Robin Kegerreis is-T rotter)

I WAS AFRAID

I was afraid to live
I was afraid to die

I was afraid
Not knowing why

I finally knew when the doctor called with the dreadful news The news no one, nor I, wanted to hear, that death was knocking at their front door

Cancer, I said, with a stream of tears

Oh no, not me-God wouldn't dare

I thought my world was coming to an end Only if I realized it was just to begin

It has taught me to love-even that much more It has taught me to give-even that much more It has taught me to laugh-even that much more

But most of all, it has taught me to live even that much more
If only that could be a gift, we all could receive and open our hearts to see
A lesson of life to be learned without death knocking at our front door

GOD
God is the answer you will see
God is always there for you and me

God won't lead us astray
He will only show us the way

It's up to you what you want to do
Live life astray or have God show you the way

I chose God, and I am glad I did
Because He has given me a life to live

THE DISEASE

One night, I was awakened from a dreadful disease

A disease I thought had taken over me
A disease of its own kind
A disease with its own mind
A disease that could take control and destroy all mankind

The disease is Cancer-the name we all know well
The name of fame that nobody wants to claim
And now it's time to put it to shame

It has taken many lives
Lives of men and women-young and old

This makes me angry-angry inside
Let's no longer run and hide

Let's take some action
Let's take some control

Let's fight the fight for all is known
Let's never give up the fight until the Cancer is gone

It's a battle that must be won
For there are many lives who survive
We are all the survivors if we take control

THE FIGHT

I was devastated at the dreadful news-that Cancer had stricken me
I knew nothing about it
And I never know how many people are fighting it

I was afraid
But I was never alone

For my family supported me every step of the way and God led me down the path every day

I am never going to give up the fight
Even when there are hopeless nights

I am not in this alone
For there are many each day who are

battling Cancer all the way

We've got to do what we know is right
And that is put up a: fight

Don't give in and don't give up Because that is what the Cancer wants

IN CONTROL

My Cancer is dying-this I know For I don't care what I am told

I don't care what the doctors tell me I don't care what the lab tests show

My Cancer is dying Because I am taking control

THE GAME

If you have had this deadly disease-Cancer
Then I am sorry to say that you have something in common with me
And I am sure you too have played the game

This Cancer is trying to take over me

CARL KEGERREIS

It's trying to beat me at its own game

    The game we call War
    The game we all must play

    What the Cancer doesn't know is I am quite a pro at this old game
    I like to win, and I will keep playing again and again Until I come out the winner in the end

    So, for all of you who have played the game and won You know as well as I do
    If the Cancer wants to play again
    You must become a pro and always win

    For those of you who are new at the game Don't get discouraged
    Because if you keep playing You too can win in the end

    So, we all have something in common Besides the disease's name

    We can all beat the Cancer at its own game of War And all come out winners

    Remember one thing

Who Is Going To Believe They Saved or Prolonged My Life

Don't pay attention to the odds-no matter what the odds Just keep playing until you come out the winner

When we all rejoice in Heaven
We will know each other not by name but when we once played the same game

I HAVE SPOKEN
This is a battle between you and me
A battle that I will win- you wait and see

Just because you have taken many lives
Doesn't mean you can take mine

You might think you're in control But when it's all over you will know
That I am the one who has taken control

I will not rest until you have been put to death
I will never let you win because you are not my friend

You are the enemy that tries to take over me But this, you see, will no longer be
Because you don't have a chance be-

tween God and me

THE VOICE

I was awakened from a voice inside me
A voice that said, "You may not flee"
A voice that said, "You must fight the fight"

A voice that said, "You must not give up day or night"
A voice that said, "You must continue to live"
A voice that reminded me of my family and friends

A voice that told me, "I could cope"
A voice that said, "There is always hope"

This voice, you see, was not me
But the beautiful voice inside me was God reaching out to me

DEAR GOD

We   ask so much from you
We ask you to always answer our prayers
We ask that you always care

We ask that you're always our friend We ask you to always lend a hand We ask that you always be there
We ask that you always take away our fears

We ask that you find a cure for all disease We ask that you help the sick and needy

We ask you to forgive our sins Then we end the prayer with Amen

In the end, what do you ask of us?
But to obey the Ten Commandments?

And it's sad to say, but not all of us do That seems so little to ask this from us After all we ask from you

MY DISEASE
I have a disease, the Doctors call it Cancer But I have another name for it
It's called "I am no longer afraid"

Ever since I found out I had Cancer My life has changed in so many ways Some might say for the worse

But I would have to say for the better I have had my ups and downs

And I have had some pain

But one lesson I have learned is to no longer be afraid

And live a full life each and every day
That is where my disease got its new name

Nobody knows what tomorrow is going to bring But don't let that stand in your way

And go out and live a full live each and every day

SURPRISE

I pad been in a hospital several times before the Cleveland Clinic. The first two times, I was seven to nine years old when I had my tonsils, adenoids, and later an appendix removed. As an adult, I was at an army hospital at Fort Ben Harrison to remove my adenoids, which had grown back. Several years later, we were with our friends to see a play at Indianapolis, Indiana, when I was taken to a local hospital with a lung virus. During the winter, I was shoveling snow and was rushed to the local hospital, believing I was having a heart attack, which, after numerous tests and several days at the hospital, proved to be nothing more than pain caused by a sore chest muscle.

Now I want you to know that I have always been a health-conscious person. I would exercise by running in the parks or walking in the railroad yards while checking the train's railroad cars. I would eat good, wholesome foods and sleep eight to nine hours a night. I did smoke cigars years ago until I was drafted into the army. I stopped smoking during the exercises at the army's military reception center.

I was required to carry a tin can and remove from the ground cigar and cigarette butts. That was enough punish ment, so I quit smoking. After I retired from the railroad, I hardly ever drank alcohol beverages, and my stress was normal. I still exercised, but I guess this Little Devil in me didn't care. I had retired as a police special agent from the CSX Transportation Railroad in December 1999 and was quite stressed losing our youngest daughter, Robin, to can cer, and my mother a year later. I received some stress when fishing. My bait would get hooked in a tree branch, or I would hook a big bass and he would get away. The Little Devil in me probably cheered. During my 2010 physical, I was reminded by Dr. Mike Applebaum, "Carl, it's time for your colonoscopy. It's been twelve years"-he looked at my medical records-"Carl, I will contact the colonoscopy center, and they will contact you."

I was contacted by the center, and I was in no hurry, so I waited until a month before my 2011 physical. I then con tacted the center requesting a date. I was sent a prescription to get the preparation to clean my colon. I contacted the center, requesting to use *a lemonade powder to mix with the preparation for a better taste-a* whole gallon-that I was required to drink, and I got their permission. The colon oscopy was completed, and I had passed it with no polyps. The center's doctor told me to return in five years. I could now see Dr. Applebaum and gleefully announce to him that I completed the colonoscopy and passed it with no polyps.

July 28, 2011, I arrived with my wife, Sandra, at Dr. Applebaum's office. Dr Applebaum is our family doctor whom we have known for many years. The doctor, good looking, with short gray hair, of medium build, and wear ing a blue medical coat greeted us and shook my hand as I bragged, "I took my colonoscopy two weeks ago, and I passed with no polyps or problems."

Dr. Applebaum smiled, sat down on a stool to write notes in my medical report, then proceeded to give me my physi cal exam. I had dropped my pants down to my groin as he checked my abdomen area. The Little Devil couldn't hide from the doctor. Moving his hand around my left side, he announced, "Carl, you have a swelling here. Have you noticed it?" He placed my hand on the swelling. I replied, "I don't feel anything different." I know the Little Devil was hiding from me because I could not- or didn't- want to feel the swelling. Dr. Applebaum gave me that glare reminding me of my dad looking at me before some punishment. "Carl, you have a swelling, and we need to get it checked. I am going to schedule you for a CT scan The X-ray Department here will contact you." We watched as he wrote the information in my medical records. After more physical tests, including a dreaded prostate exam, I left the office wondering and con corned. Several days before the CT scan and x-ray, I would check my abdomen and still could not feel any swelling as that Little Devil I believe continued to hide. I would tell Sandra nothing to worry about although I still wondered.

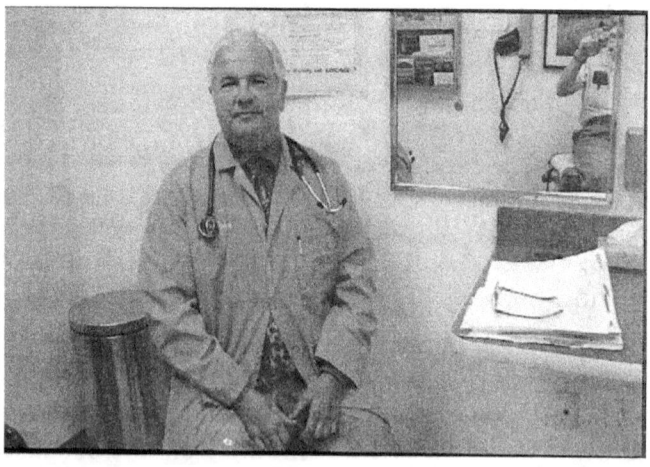

Dr. Michael S. Applebaum at the West Toledo Internal Medicine Associates 7640 W. Sylvania Ave., Suite 1, Sylvania, Ohio, June 11, 2012.

I was contacted by the CT scan and X-ray Departments. I had received a barium drink from the X-ray Department and was told to drink it prior to the CT scan August 2, 2011, the day arrived for my CT scan, and I sat with my wife in the waiting room, which seemed like hours. My name was called, and I followed the woman technician who had long blonde hair, in her late thirties, wearing a white medical jacket. We arrived in this room that contained a small platform centered in front of a large funny-looking machine. She requested that I remove my slacks and handed me a medical gown and left the room. She soon returned and requested that I lie on the platform and place my arms and hands above my head. I was on the platform, moving into the circle front of the machine. I was still wonder ing but thought maybe I had bumped my left side, which had caused the swelling, and I begin smiling knowing this machine would prove it. Over the speaker on the machine, I heard, "Carl, take a deep breath, hold it, let it out slowly, now take a deep breath and hold it."

I complied several times, watching my body being absorbed in the machine's mouth while it circled the plat form similar to the second hand on a watch. That was it, I was done. I jumped off the platform, got dressed, satis fied-"nothing more than a bump and bruise." I had to ask the technician, "Did the x-ray show a swelling?"

She smiled, replying, "Your doctor will look at the pictures and discuss them with you."

Sandra and I talked about the CT scan on the way home, and I assured her there was nothing to worry about as I felt great and I had probably bumped my side, which caused the swelling. I was still trying not to be nervous, but I must admit I was apprehensive.

The morning of August 3 was a surprise. The phone rang, and someone from Dr. Applebaum's office was telling me, "The doctor wants to see you at 3:00 p.m. today before he leaves the office to talk with you about your CT scan."

I asked, "Is it serious?"

The reply was, "The doctor wants to see you at 3:00 p.m.

Today.

I replied, "Okay, I will be there." Satisfied it probably was nothing, I looked at my wife, Sandra, telling her, "That was someone from Dr. Applebaum's office, and we need to see the doctor at 3:00 p.m. today. We are going to find out that I bumped and bruised the left side of my abdomen. Nothing to be concerned about."

I was no longer wondering but was very nervous as we met with Dr. Applebaum, who had a concerned look, speaking, "Carl, we got your CT scan back, and your swell ing was caused by a liposarcoma." I was hoping to hear from Dr. Applebaum that the swelling was caused by a bump and a muscle was bruised-but a liposarcoma! "Carl, I am going to contact a very conservative surgeon here in Toledo who will check you, read the CT scan and determine what he believes should be done.

I started asking many questions. "Dr. Applebaum, what. 1s a lipo ... sarcoma?

The doctor shook his head, replying, "It's a fat cell tis sue that grows in the abdomen. It might be malignant or benign."

"Dr. Applebaum, this sarcoma, I will call the... Little Devil." We both laughed and Sandra smiled. "Is this what caused my swelling on the left side of my abdomen? Why didn't I have any symptoms? How long have I had this sarcoma? Is it malignant or benign? Will this cause any other complications?"

The doctor shook his head, sitting on the stool. "Carl, I am referring you to see a Toledo surgeon who will answer your questions and only perform surgery if he believes it's necessary."

The doctor wrote more notes in my medical file as I asked, "Dr. Applebaum, what happens if I choose not to have surgery?"

I swear I could hear the Little Devil laughing as the doctor replied, "Carl, the sarcoma could be benign or malignant and will certainly create extreme serious prob lems for you if you do nothing." The doctor wrote addi tional notes in my file then handed me a disc containing my CT scan pictures, telling me, "Carl, take this disc to the surgeon who will contact you." He shook my hand, wishing me and Sandra the best and assuring me I needed to see the surgeon. The doctor left the room, and I looked at my wife, "Honey, I wonder what the next surprise will be?" Well, I wasn't a basket case yet, but I was getting more apprehend sive. We returned to the car, and Sandra kissed me, speak ing, "Honey, everything will be okay." It was a quite ride home. Now you must understand that raised as a preacher's kid, I always believed in prayer. Every night I would pray for all our families' health and give thanks for all our blessings. As I drove the car home, I began praying with my eyes open. Yep, you guessed right. I was praying for God to remove the Little Devil from my abdomen. I was get ting some movement in my abdomen. I believe the Little Devil was trying to hide. I had seen on television some of the religious healing shows. The minister would pray for the healing and shout, "Demon, leave this man, leave this woman, or leave this child." That is how I got the idea to refer to my liposarcoma as the Little Devil.

MORE SURPRISES

I had almost forgotten about my problem with the Little Devil. I was enjoying riding my lawn tractor, cutting the grass in the backyard, when Sandra had answered the phone. Looking toward our deck, I saw my wife motioning to me from the deck door and hollering. I turned off the engine, removed my ear covers, and heard, "Honey, some one from the Toledo surgeon's office is on the phone." As I hopped off the tractor, walking toward the deck, I was hop ing that the person on the phone was tired of waiting and no longer wanted to talk to me. No such luck, as I heard, "Carl, Dr. Applebaum called our office requesting that you see our doctor. I have an appointment for you on August 19, 2011, Friday morning at 10:50 a.m. Please bring with you all your medications and the CT scan disc."

I replied, "Thank you." Hanging up the phone, I turned to see the love of my life of forty-nine years looking at me while I wrote the date and time on our calendar, speak ing, "Honey, we have to see the surgeon on Friday, August 19, at 10:50 a.m." I returned to mowing the yard, wonder ing why this is happening to me. I had remembered asking my father, who was in an Indianapolis Hospital lying in a bed and being treated for cancer of the lymph nodes, dur ing

July 1986. I asked, "Dad, why you-a minister who has always helped his fellow man and believed and preached God's holy gospel-why would you be in here with can cer?" Dad grabbed my hand, smiled, and told me, "Son, I am a human." He didn't have to say another word as I understood, attempting to hold back my tears. Two weeks later, Dad went to God's kingdom. I believe he had a lipo sarcoma, as Dad had a similar swelling on the right side of his abdomen.

Sometime later, the doctors told me the liposarcoma is genetic, rare, and I wondered, *is this what Dad had in the Indianapolis Hospital, and I had inherited it from him?*

August 19 arrived too soon. We walked into the sur geon's office. I gave the young woman my insurance card, my co-paycheck, and the CT scan disc. We sat in the wait ing room with several other people. I started talking with one patient who appeared younger than myself but looked older with partial bald gray hair, thin, with a smile, while Sandra talked to his wife. He continued smiling, telling me that this Toledo surgeon was the best, saved his life, and assured me I was in the right place. I thanked him when my name was called, and a woman nurse wearing a white jacket ushered us into an examination room. She checked my weight, 190 pounds, my height, six feet, telling us, "The doctor will see you as soon as he reviews your CT scan disc." I slowly walked back and forth in the room, wonder ing what the doctor is going to tell me. I swear I could hear the Little Devil laughing.

A few minutes passed, which seemed like an hour, when the door opened, and the doctor walked in the room. The doctor was my height, six feet, about my weight, 190 pounds, in his fifties, and he examined my abdomen. Smiling, he grabbed my hand, placing it below my left ribcage, asking, "Carl, do you feel the swelling?"

Pushing downward, I nodded yes, because for the first time I finally admitted to myself have it. I couldn't believe it. I have a liposarcoma.

The doctor took my pulse, checked my breathing, and checked my neck for swollen lymph nodes. "Carl, have you had any problems with this swelling, which we believe is a liposarcoma?"

I shook my head, explaining, "Nothing serious, just the usual burping, occasional acid reflux, and passing gas."

The doctor, smiling, continued talking. "Sometimes a liposarcoma will cause those problems. I haven't been able to see your CT scan but the Radiology Department's direc tive is reporting you have a liposarcoma and indicating it's huge. Checking your swelling in your abdomen has con firmed that it's large. I will need to review the CT scan and get back with you. Do you or your wife have any questions?" I looked at Sandra then at the doctor, asking, "Have you ever removed a liposarcoma from the abdomen?"

"Carl, I recently removed one from a younger man who had a smaller sarcoma compared to yours. He recently had a CT scan, and it is growing again. He will require another surgery."

Hearing that, I now understood what if felt like being between a rock and a hard place as I asked, "I have never had any serious problems with this liposarcoma, so what can it do to me?" Observing the doctor's expression, I remarked, "I guess that was a dumb question, right?"

The Doctor shook his head with a very concerned look, replying, "Carl, most of these sarcomas are malig nant. The swelling in your abdomen is large. I need to review your CT scan to determine if I should perform the surgery, or you might want to consider the James Cancer Center in Columbus, Ohio, or the Michigan University Hospital. I will let you know what I have decided by tomorrow."

I asked, "Doctor, what causes this ... liposarcoma?" He replied, "It's rare and believed genetic."

I said to myself, Yep, *I got the Little Devil from Dad.* We thanked the doctor and headed for home. Driving home, I kept repeating like a broken record, "You've got to be kidding me. I don't believe what's happening."

The following day, the call arrived with the surgeon's nurse telling me, "Carl, the doctor has reviewed your CT. scan and believes you should contact the James Cancer Center at Columbus, Ohio. He will not consider surgery here." I thanked her and collapsed in my chair. I could swear I heard the Little Devil laughing and bragging, "I've got you. You're mine." Sandra looked at me, and I stood up, hugging her, telling her about the call and that everything would be okay.

Several days passed, and I was in no hurry to contact any cancer center. It's so hard to explain your feelings when you realize that you have a cancer that is slowly growing. So, I continue with prayers, doing research, thinking and believing that the correct answer to my problem is to leave it alone. I know the Little Devil was agreeing with me, as my abdomen would rumble, and I would pass gas and burp.

I was reading this article in a medical magazine about cancer tumors. It reported, "To stop a tumor, eat broccoli, cabbage, Bok choy, cauliflower, Brussels sprouts, and mustard." Yep, you guessed it. The grocery cart was filled with those ingredients, and I started on a new diet. Sandra fixed the food for every dinner. I was putting mustard on my broccoli and Brussels sprouts.

The taste was a little rough, but I soon adjusted to the taste, and it became a pleasure when I believe I could hear the Little Devil choke. I soon grew accustomed to eating those foods at every dinner meal. At a restaurant, I would order broccoli and smother it with mustard. Sandra would continue to cook those foods, and I would eat them. However, I never felt any different or better, and I begin to believe the Little Devil was on to me, so I called the James Cancer Center. The appointment was made for us on August 25, 2011, at the cancer center at Columbus, Ohio, to visit their surgeon. I had contacted our supplement medical insurance to determine if the insurance company was in network with the James Cancer Center. There was an insurance problem, so I canceled the appointment and felt a rumble in my abdomen. I believe the Little Devil was happy, jumping up and down. While working on the CSX Transportation Railroad as the police division chief in Columbus, Ohio, policing the Railroad at Cleveland, Ohio, was under my supervision, so I was aware of the Cleveland Clinic. I contacted the Clinic, who reported that they covered our insurance. An appointment was set for August 29, 2011, to visit Surgeon Dr. Bipan Chand. We traveled to the Cleveland Clinic.

My first impression arriving at the Clinic was looking at Sandra, saying, "Wow, what a huge place. "The best way to describe it is a city surrounded by a city.

This parking garage is located across from the clinic's Sydell & Arnold Miller Family Pavilion Hospital, May 22, 2012.

The Sydell & Arnold Miller Family Pavilion Hospital, May 22, 2012.

Euclid Avenue, the clinic's medical buildings, their cam pus, shops, and restaurants, May 22, 2012.

The clinic's Crile Building, May 22, 2012.

A Cleveland Clinic shuttle bus is picking up patients at the side entrance of the Sydell & Arnold Miller Family Pavilion Hospital, May 22, 2012.

THANK YOU, GOD, FOR DOCTORS, NURSES, AND THE CLEVELAND CLINIC

I thank God every day for our blessings, for our friends and family. Sometimes we overlook important people such as doctors and nurses. We get sick; we have doctors and nurses who are educated, trained, and continue learning new medical techniques to help us.

We approached the Cleveland Clinic's main building after departing a huge parking garage and crossing a busy Euclid Avenue. I looked at Sandra, speaking, "We are here. Wow, what a huge place!" We entered through the moving glass doors, walking down the long hallway, passing an escalator loaded with doctors, nurses, and people disappearing below us. Later, we discovered the escalator would take you downstairs where you walked in a tunnel under Euclid Avenue to the clinic's parking garage.

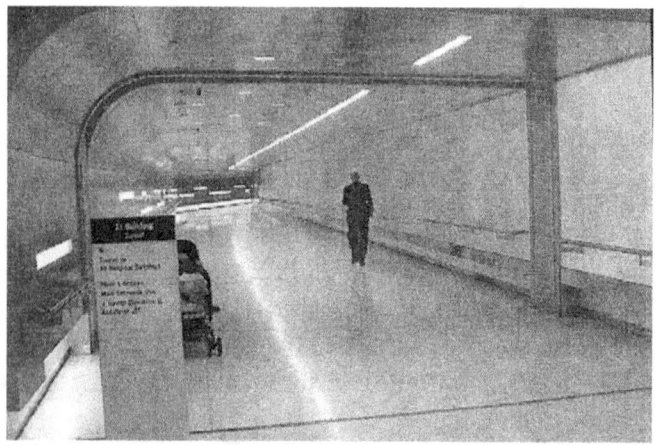

The tunnel is available to walk from the Sydell & Arnold Miller Family Pavilion Hospital under Euclid Avenue to the clinic's parking garage, May 22, 2012.

The elevators from the clinic's tunnel to the parking garage, May 22, 2012.

The escalator from the tunnel to the Sydell & Arnold Miller Family Pavilion Hospital for children and adults, May 22, 2012.

The cafeteria, which includes a McDonald's, Subway, a huge salad bar with various entrees in the Sydell &Arnold Miller Family Pavilion Hospital, May 22, 2012.

Entering a huge open area, we noticed several people wearing red jackets, talking to many people. We talked with an older man in a red jacket with white hair but par tially bald, wearing glasses, and with a beaming smile, who requested, "Can I help you?" I showed him the letter sent to me from the Cleveland Clinic with my appointment to see Dr. Bipan Chand. He walked with us to an elevator, telling us the correct floor to exit, and we arrived in a large room with a hallway where people were in a line waiting to check in with the desk receptionist. The receptionist told us to go to their waiting room.

The room was filled with several men and women. Some we're waiting in wheelchairs. Soon my name was called by a young nurse, who ushered us down a long hallway into an examination room. She took my weight and height measurement and pulse, telling us, "Dr. Bipan Chand will be with you shortly." I began pacing the floor back and forth in the room, wondering what's the next surprise. The nurse left the room as a Dr. Kevin El-Hayek entered the room. (See his picture in the chapter "Did We Get the Little Devil?")

Dr. El-Hayek showed us the Little Devil revealed on the CT scan disc I had brought with me from Toledo. The Little Devil was round, huge, and the doctor pointed to the left side of the picture, explaining, "This is a liposarcoma, and it's huge. It will require surgery. Dr. Bipan Chand will soon be here."

Dr. Chand entered the examination room. He was sur prised seeing me. I believe he thought I would be heavier. (See his picture in the chapter "Did We Get the Little Devil?") The doctor was smiling, which made me feel bet ter. He checked my abdomen and told me, "This liposar coma will require surgery." Demonstrating, he moved his hand, indicating an incision from my breastbone to my groin. Our son, Rob, arrived, and I felt great that he was with us.

I began with the questions. "Dr. Chand, I researched this liposarcoma on the Internet and found it can be malig nant or benign. How will we know if it's malignant?"

Dr. Chand replied, "Carl, when we remove it during your surgery, we will do a biopsy then we will know. Normally, a liposarcoma is a slow-growing malignant tumor. As big as your tumor is, it probably has been growing in your Abdo men for some time. Did you notice any problems?"

I replied, "Burping, gas, and acid reflux."

"Carl, we have removed several malignant tumors like yours, and after the surgery we use radiation by our Oncology Department."

"Dr. Chand, what will happen if I don't have the surgery?" Dr. Chand, still smiling, spoke, "Due to the size of your liposarcoma, we may have to remove your left kidney during your surgery."

I didn't ask any more questions, as my whole body was shaking, and I felt miserable. I believe I heard the Little

Devil crying after I agreed to the surgery. An appointment was made for me on September 16, 2011, for pre surgery tests. We left the examination room, and I now had to find Dr. Kevin Stephans in the Oncology Department. We were walking toward the elevators, and I was thinking about my childhood. I always had a desire to be a policeman. I remember at ten years old I had a friend whose dad was an Indiana state trooper. I would try to be at my friend's house to see his dad when he arrived home in his police car, in uniform, with that big gun hanging on his hip. Every time I saw him, I would ask this question: "Have you ever shot anyone?" His reply was always a smile, and he would shake his head. I didn't know if that was a yes or no, so I guessed he had shot several bad guys. I also remember hearing on the radio about the US government Secret Service Agency who protects the United States president. So, I wrote a letter to the Secret Service in Washington DC. Every day right after school, I was at the local post office checking for that special envelope, and each time the postman would tell me, "Sorry, son, there is no mail for you."

It was on a Saturday when I arrived at the post office, and the postman handed me a letter. Man, it was like being in a candy store. I slowly opened the envelope, and a card fell to the floor. I picked up the card, read it, and the letter told me I am now a junior Secret Service agent. Boy, everyone saw that card- my parents, my brothers, my paper customers, our church members, and even my 4-H Rabbits.

I guess I was predestined to be a policeman. Thank you, God, for doctors and nurses.

I had a close friend in elementary school, and when we played together all he ever talked about was that he had to be a doctor. I had to be a policeman. I guess he was pre destined to be a doctor. He had graduated from Indiana University and went on to medical school. The last time I visited with him was at the university, but I believe God had predestined him to be a doctor. We arrived at the Oncology Department to see Dr. Stephans. Again, I checked in with the desk receptionist and was told to wait in the wait ing room. She told us, "Dr. Stephans's nurse will be with you shortly."

A nurse called my name, and we soon were in an examination room waiting for Dr. Kevin Stephans. After the nurse took my height, weight, and pulse, the door opened; and a smiling Dr. Stephans-medium build, tall, with a receding hairline-greeted us with a handshake. He sat down in front of a computer showing us the Little Devil's picture and talking with us about it. He pulled from the drawer a plastic item, circular in design. Smiling, he told us, "This device is silicone similar to a silicon device we will place in your abdomen after the liposarcoma is removed. We have used this method in the clinic since 2009. This device with catheters will be placed in your abdomen during surgery, and the following morning we will take you to our oncology room to receive the radiation . You will return to surgery, and the silicon device with the catheters will be removed."

    I looked at the floor shaking my head, then at my wife Sandra, attempting to smile. I must tell you I felt miser able and nervous as we left the examination room returning to the central lobby. I felt better seeing the people in wheel chairs; using canes, crutches; getting their friendly attention from the clinic staff and was I surprised that morn ing by our daughter Carla and her husband, Michael, who called the motel and paid our bill before we checked out.

    My first trip to the Cleveland Clinic, boy, was I impressed with the love and friendship extended to us and our kids from their doctors, nurses, and staff I felt good as we took the escalator to the tunnel, and the elevator to the parking lot. Guess what happened as we were leaving the parking lot? No, I had the parking ticket, but drove into the wrong exit lane. The cashier stopped us, hollering, "You're in the wrong lane!"

Embarrassed, I tried to hand her my ticket with money, but she smiled and motioned for us to continue out the exit doors. Leaving the parking garage, I said to Sandra, "The people are nice in the clinic and even in the parking garage."

So embarrassed with other cars behind me, I learned how to exit their parking garage. September 16, 2011, arrived too soon, and I and Sandra returned to the Cleveland Clinic for pre surgery tests. My day began in a laboratory where the clinic technicians took my blood. I had inter views at the Radiation-Oncology Department; took tests at two Internal Medicine Departments, admitting hospital interviews, and preoperative clearance papers I had to sign for surgery and radiation. I visited a doctor for an anesthesia evaluation and Dr. Bipan Chand with his associate Kevin El-Hayek. Everyone laughed when I referred to my sarcoma as the Little Devil. This had been an experience with the doctors, nurses, and staff who were so friendly, always with smiles. I have to tell you, I had no desire to do the pre surgery, but after it was completed, I felt good being there at the clinic with these wonderful people. However, I was not looking forward to my next appointment on September 22, 2011, for surgery.

I noticed that the Little Devil was quiet and not mov ing around. I believe he was hiding. September 22, 2011, arrived, and I found myself at the Cleveland Clinic with my wife, Sandra, and our son, Rob. I was directed to the preparation room and told to remove all clothes and put on a surgery gown. I was nervous and began wondering, *Will I soon be at the pearly gates in heaven?* No, that can't happen as I don't want to leave my wife, Sandra; her dad, who is alone, ninety-four; my family; my grandchildren; and my friends.

A smiling nurse asked, "Carl, would you like to have a chaplain with you before we take you to surgery?" Lying on the stretcher hooked up with an IV in my wrist, I nodded yes, replying, "Yes, thank you."

Baptist chaplain Charissa Prunty arrived smiling. She visited with us and then, holding my hand, offered a beautiful prayer for my well-being. I must tell you right then a warm feeling engulfed my body, and I was no longer nervous. I kissed my wife, said good-bye to my son, and I was being pushed in the hallway.

Entering this first huge room with curtains, I sat up on the stretcher, while several nurses and technicians placed a needle in my spine to help my surgery pain. That warm feeling was with me as I was pushed into the operating room, while whispering the Lord's Prayer. I moved myself from the stretcher to the operating table. A mask was placed over my face, and I was requested to breathe deep. Hours later I was pushed into a room where I saw the love of my life, Sandra; our son, Rob; and my brother Bob. I knew I was okay, and the Little Devil was gone. So, I went to sleep thanking God. The clinic staff brought a roll-away bed to our room for Sandra. Yep, you're wondering if I crossed through the tunnel to a heavenly life while I was in surgery for six hours. There are many books written about people who were declared dead, crossed over to the heavenly life, then returned to their human life talking about their experience. There are stories about people traveling in a special, long, beautiful white tunnel while watching their lives as a child, teenager, or adult pass before them. They arrive at the end of the tunnel to meet angels, spiritual family members, or friends who have died and who tell them their time to die is not now and that they must return to their human lives. I must tell you while I was in surgery, I don't recall any heaven experience. I didn't feel any pain during my surgery. I thank the anesthetist doctor and the surgeons for taking care of me.

Arriving back to my room number J83-21 after the surgery, I saw Sandra, Rob, and Bob, which was like being in heaven. I still had that warm feeling in my body I had received from that prayer in the surgery preparation room. September 23, 2011, the nurses and staff moved me from my bed to a stretcher where I was rolled to the Oncology Department. I was placed in a room with a metal robot, like a robot I had seen years ago in a scientific movie. The catheters extending from my abdomen were attached to the robot's face. I could hear a whirling noise coming from the robot. Someone reported from a speaker that I was now receiving radiation. The radiation was stopped, and the catheters were removed from the robot. I was moved from the room and returned to surgery to remove the silicon device and catheters from my abdomen. My incision was stapled, supported with gauze, tape, and a tube was protruding from my abdomen connected to a small plastic bottle used for fluid drainage. I was returned to my room where I stayed two weeks.

The surgery and radiation had created bile

in my digestive system. A male nurse was busy placing an irrigation tube in my mouth, down my throat, and into my stomach.

He was shocked when I told him after I had gagged numerous times, "Thank you." Smiling, he replied, "Carl, you are the first patient that has ever thanked me for putting an irrigation tube in their body." I looked at him, attempt ing to smile while watching the bile leaving my stomach by moving through the tube extending from my nose with help from an electric pump behind my bed.

It was my third day after the second surgery when a therapy technician walked into my room with a walker. What a site to behold. Yep, there I was in a gown, covered by my robe, with cloth slippers on my feet, with all the IV attachments, including the irrigation tube extending from my nose, and now walking in the clinic's hallway with the assistance from the technician.

I had told you in this book's foreword about my guardian angel. I will never forget Tuesday, September 27, 2011, at 3:30 a.m. I heard a small noise, and raising myself in bed, I looked at the wall clock. There was a beautiful glowing light that I have never seen before in front of my bed. The colors were light gold and raspberry red. I looked at the light then looked at the other bed where

Sandra was asleep. I knew this was not a dream. I started to lie down when I heard a quiet but a penetrating voice. "Carl, do you remember when you were called to the Ministry at the Methodist Youth Camp at Epworth Forest? Do you remember the quiet night during the youth service? No one was to talk to each other until the next day. Carl, do you remember the girl who approached you telling you that God wanted you to be a minister. This was your calling from God."

I wanted to pull the blankets over my head to hide. I remembered the girl. I had reminded her we weren't to. talk to each other until in the morning. The following morning, I talked with her, and she had denied talking to me. I had always wanted to be a policeman.

The voice continued, "Carl, you have lived a life fulfilled as you wished. Will you help other people who may have your disease in their body? Will you tell the people about your experience, where they can receive medical help, and have this disease removed from their bodies? Will you explain about God's love to family, friends-new friends and old friends?" Again, I looked at my wife, who was asleep, and this amazing picture appeared on the wall below the clock. The voice continued, "Carl, use this picture to show an angel to illustrate God's love for Family, Friends, New Friends, Old Friends. and all People. The angel is shown on the book cover.

The picture disappeared with that beautiful light in front of my bed. I had not received any pain pills recently or any other medications that would cause me to hallucinate. I looked around the room, my wife was still sleeping; the clock on the wall was still showing 3:30 a.m. I know that I was not dreaming, and my guardian angel had talked to me. I wish I had told the angel, "Thank you for all the times you have helped me. I began thinking, *is this why I am here at the clinic? Is this happening to me because I didn't become a minister?* I then remembered what Dad had told me when he was in the Indianapolis Hospital-that we are *humans*.

DID WE GET THE LITTLE DEVIL?

Dr. Bipan Chand and associate doctor Kevin El-Hayek. Authorized picture sent to author by Dr. Kevin El-Hayek, February 26, 2013.

Dr. Kevin L. Stephans, Oncology Department, Cleveland Clinic, talking with us in the clinic's examination room, May 22, 2012.

Wow, the Cleveland Clinic is a great hospital. Two weeks it took to recover from the surgery at the hospital, and I must tell you about the wonderful care I had received from the doctors, nurses, and staff. Thanks to all the clinic's people who assisted us during my recovery, as I have never been in a hospital where Dr. Charles, Dr. Gibson, and several clinic's associate doctors checked on me every morning. Dr. Bipan Chand and associate doctor Kevin El-Hayek would check on me each evening. The doctors, nurses, technicians, the clinic staff's friendship, and their instructions all helped me to recover quickly. A special thanks to the Nutrition Department, which kept me on a liquid diet, and the hospital kitchen staff who prepared my meals.

October 6, 2011, during the afternoon, I was discharged from the hospital. My brother Bob and our son, Rob, took us home. We traveled from the clinic to the Hilton Homewood Suites to pick up our car. A special thanks to the hotel manager and staff for their hospitality to our family. It was great to be home, thanks to my brother Bob and our son, Rob.

The recovery at home was slow, as warned by Dr. Bipari Chand telling me that it could take several months. I still had the drainage bottle attached to my abdomen, and I was requested to keep a record of the fluid each time I emptied the bottle. The clinic nutrition staffs had asked me if I would need anyone to visit our home to provide me with nutrition by IV or extra therapy. I felt I was fortunate that I didn't require any special care at home, so I begin my own recovery. Now you're probably wondering how I did that after having a cancer tumor the size of a soccer ball removed from my abdomen during surgery and then radiation. I had lost twenty-eight pounds, could hardly walk, was dizzy when standing or after sitting, but I was determined, and this is what I did! I started on a high-calorie diet to include Ensure-"a chocolate nutrition shake"-that I had received in the clinic every meal. I started walking from our backyard deck to the front porch several times during the day. I would sit on the porch then continue my walk around the house returning to the deck. I did this for a couple of weeks then graduated toward attempting to walk in a store. It was not easy. I hung on to the shopping cart then, finding a bench or chair, sat for a few minutes, but I was determined; and I, with the help of the shopping cart, was walking around the store. I then graduated to walking in a retail warehouse, first with a shopping cart and finally no shopping cart. I really got brave and talked Sandra into walking with me in the park. I begin to feel better each day while I was slowly gain ing weight. October 13, 2011, my brother Bob returned us to the Cleveland Clinic for my post-operation checkup with Dr. Bipan Chand. This was a nice surprise seeing Dr. Chand, his associate doctor Kevin El-Hayek, with Dr. Gibson and Dr. Charles. The tube protruding from my abdomen to the drainage bottle was removed. Yes, I hollered "Ouch!" It was nice not having the bottle pinned to my shorts or having to keep a log on the drainage in the bottle. It was great seeing all the doctors together so we could thank each one for saving my life. I was surprised when I was told, "Carl, we haven't saved your life, we have prolonged it."

Dr. Chand, satisfied with my recovery, scheduled me for a CT scan at the clinic on February 17, 2012. I was concerned, asking, "Will this Little Devil return?"

Dr. Chand, smiling, replied, "We hope that the radiation stopped it, but your sarcoma was huge."

I remembered what the Toledo surgeon had told me about his patient's sarcoma had returned. We thanked the doctors and left the clinic. Arriving at home, I continued my recovery with the Ensure, a high-calorie diet, and walking. I would walk around our neighborhood with Sandra. I was feeling better every day and believed the Little Devil was gone forever. February 17, 2012, arrived, and I was apprehensive about returning to the Cleveland Clinic for a CT scan I had received a letter from the clinic explaining that Dr. Bipan Chand had left the clinic. Later, I discovered that Dr. Bipan Chand was the director for Loyola's Center for Metabolic Surgery and Bariatric Care at Maywood, Illinois. I was scheduled to see · Dr. Kevin Stephans and Dr. Sricharan Chalikonda after my CT scan. We arrived, and I was ushered into the CT scan room after drinking a bottle of barium, wearing a gown with an IV attached to my left arm to check my right kidney. I no longer had a left kidney, thanks to the Little Devil. The CT scan was completed, my IV was removed, and we thanked the technicians and left to see Dr. Stephans.

00000

Doctor Stephans pointed to a small, circular tissue on my left bowel discovered by my new CT scan shown on his computer. He looked at me, speaking, "Carl, this could be another liposarcoma that is small now, or it could be your body tissue."

I thought, *Oh no the Little Devil has a friend who has attached its body to my bowel.*

I looked at Dr. Stephans, asking, "Will this require another surgery and radiation? Do I have any other options?" Again, he pointed at the circular tissue in the picture, replying, "It's small and would be easier to remove now before it gets larger. Are you scheduled to see Dr. Chalikonda today?"

I shook my head yes, asking, "Do we have to do this now, or can we wait and determine if it's growing?"

Dr. Stephans replied, "Dr. Chalikonda will determine if the surgery is necessary. I will talk with him."

I continued looking at the picture of my CT scan on his computer screen wondering if the Little Devil is going to win this battle. I guess before the surgery, he had left a friend to continue to destroy my body. I asked, "If I have to have another surgery, will it require a silicon device with catheters for radiation and another surgery to remove it?" Dr. Stephans looked at us smiling, replying, "We now do not use the silicon device. A technique is now used with a new radiation machine that points the radiation to the required part of your body." I was still concerned and nervous but thankful I would only require one surgery if it was necessary. We thanked Dr. Stephans and left the Oncology Department and walked along the clinic campus to the Crile Building for my appointment with Dr. Sricharan Chalikonda. I was nervous wondering what this Little Devil's friend was going to do to my body. The Cleveland Clinic letter I had received explained Dr. Bipan Chand had left the clinic and now required an appointment for me with surgeon Dr. Chalikonda. I had researched Dr. Chalikonda on the Internet and discovered the doctor had practiced in Pittsburgh, Pennsylvania. I located his picture, his education records, his medical practicing background, and the remarks from his patients, which were great. I felt good knowing this information about Dr. Chalikonda before meeting him.

We arrived at the patient's waiting room in the clinic's Crile Building. I checked in with the receptionist, gave her my co-pay, and waited in the patient's area. A nurse arrived, called my name, and took my pulse, temperature, height, and weight.

Who Is Going To Believe They Saved or Prolonged My Life

Dr. Sricharan Chalikonda, Dr. Au Bui, and registered nurse Lisa Taylor in the examination room at the clinic's Crile Building, May 22, 2012.

Dr. Chalikonda's patient's wa1tmg room m the Crile Building, Cleveland Clinic, May 22, 2012.

Associate doctor Au Bui entered the room (see his picture for description) and showed us the CT scan on their computer. He talked with us about surgery to remove my tissue found on my bowel. I asked, "Will this surgery cause me to have to live with catheters and a bowel bag?"

Dr. Au Bui explained how the tissue would be removed during surgery from my bowel by drawing pictures for us to see. His explaining the procedure helped me feel some what better. Dr. Chalikonda entered the room with his nurse, Lisa Taylor. (See their pictures for description.) He talked with Dr. Au Bui then told us, "Carl, I have reviewed your CT scan and I have talked with Dr. Kevin Stephans. We have three choices. The first choice is to use a needle biopsy to determine if that tissue on your bowel is malig nant. The second choice is surgery to remove the tissue with a biopsy. The third choice will be yours, Carl-to do nothing now and return in three months for another CT scan to determine if the tissue has grown. It the tissue is larger, we will perform the surgery, with a biopsy, and if the tissue is malignant, we will use radiation. So, Carl, what is your choice?"

You have heard the expression, "Damn if you do and damn if you don't." I looked at my wife, Sandra, then at Dr. Chalikonda, asking, "If I wait three months having the CT scan and it indicates the tissue has grown, will you still be able to remove the tissue and won't explain to me that nothing can be done?"

Dr. Chalikonda, smiling, answered, "We can remove it now or later. This sarcoma is normally a slow-growing tumor, but it's your decision."

Looking at both doctors, I said, "I will wait."

We were leaving the examination room when Dr. Chalikonda instructed his nurse to make an appointment for another CT scan in three months. I shook hands with both doctors, thanking them. Driving home, I had decided the Little Devil is gone, and maybe that tissue on my bowel is not his friend. However, I sent messages on the computer to all our family and friends telling them about my new experience and asking for their prayers. I continued at home with exercising; eating cabbage, broccoli with mustard, bok choy, cauliflower, Brussels sprouts, mustard, and added eggplant to my diet. May 22, 2012, arrived, and once again we are returning to the Cleveland Clinic for a new CT scan which will determine if the Little Devil's friend has grown.

THE LITTLE DEVIL'S FRIEND

Cleveland Clinic registered nurses Mary Hodakievic and Gwendolyn Ferguson at the clinic's CT scan center, May 22, 2012.

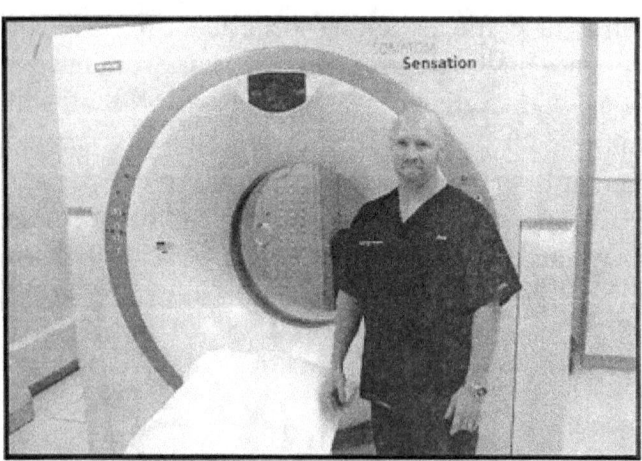

Cleveland Clinic technician Joshua Carnes standing beside the CT scan machine at the center, May 22, 2012.

Who Is Going To Believe They Saved or Prolonged My Life

We arrived at the Cleveland Clinic on May 22, 2012; I took several pictures with my camera because I want you to see the clinic. My day started at the CT scan center, drinking the barium, sitting in the waiting area with many people. I: finished the barium and was directed to a small room with a locker. I disrobed placing my clothes in the locked locker, returning to the waiting area, where I was directed to the CT scan center and met nurses Mary Hodakievic and Gwendolyn Ferguson (see pictures for description). An IV was placed in my left arm to check my right kidney.

The nurse did a great job. It didn't hurt and it was quick.

I was directed to the CT scan machine by technician Joshua Carnes (see picture for description). The CT scan was completed, and we arrived at the Oncology Department to see Dr. Kevin Stephans. Nurse Samantha Brigotti escorted us to the examination room checking my pulse, weight, and temperature. Dr. Stephans entered the room smiling and showed us my CT scan picture on their computer screen. Wow, the circular tissue believed to be another sarcoma on my bowel had shrunk. Dr. Stephans pointed at the tissue, telling us, "Carl, I don't know what you have been doing, but keep it up." I replied, "I believe it's because my family and friends have been praying for me. "I didn't tell him how many times each day I was praying. I continued, "The tissue is shrinking, not growing. So do I need surgery and radiation?"

Dr. Stephans smiled, replying, "I believe you will need another CT scan for us to look at it again. I will talk to Dr. Chalikonda. What you are doing is great and working, so keep it up." I looked at Sandra, smiling, and raised my head thanking God. We shook hands with Dr. Stephans and left to see D r. Chalikonda.

Associate doctor Au Bui and nurse Lisa Taylor arrived in the examination room with Dr. Chalikonda, who appeared surprised and told us, "The CT scan looks good. The tissue has shrunk. We need to see you again in another three months."

I replied, "Three more months and then I will graduate and be free from the Little Devil and his friends, I hope."

Dr. Chalikonda replied, "Carl, keep doing what you have been doing. We will see you in three months."

I arrived back home and felt great knowing that this circular tissue on my bowel that I have called "the Little Devil's friend" had shrunk. So, I continued with the same diet, exercise, and prayer.

The Cleveland Clinic contacted me with a

new appointment for September 11, 2012. Boy, that past three months went fast, and we returned to the clinic for another CT scan. It was a quiet drive to Cleveland, Ohio, on the Ohio Turnpike, and I continued thinking, *Why is this happening?* I had almost forgotten that I am a *human*. We arrived at the clinic's CT scan center, where I went through the same process as three months ago. We then went to see Dr. Kevin Stephans in the Oncology Department. Nurse Samantha Brigotti (see picture for description) checked my weight, pulse, temperature, and escorted us to the examination room. Associate doctor Monica Shukla (see picture for description) entered the room and showed us my CT scan on their computer screen. Yes, there it was-that circular tissue, which was still shrinking. Boy, was I happy. The doctor showed us a CT scan picture of my right lung. She pointed to a small, circular nodule that was visible, telling us it could be another sarcoma from that huge Little Devil removed from my abdomen. I looked at Sandra, shaking my head, asking, "Could a sarcoma grow in my lung from the malignant sarcoma that was removed from my abdomen during surgery last year?"

The doctor replied, "Yes, that can happen."

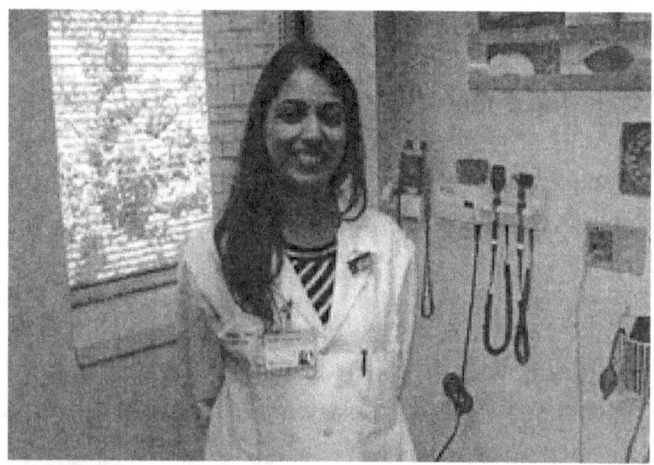

Dr. Monica Shukla, the clinic's Radiation-Oncology Department, September 11, 2012.

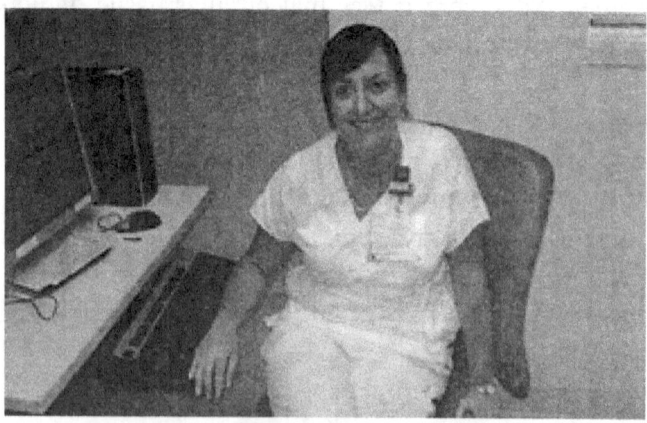

Registered nurse Samantha Brigotti, the clinic's Radiation-Oncology Department, September 11, 2012.

Who Is Going To Believe They Saved or Prolonged My Life

I put my head in my hands thinking the Little Devil has placed his first friend on my bowel and another friend in my lung. How many other friends has he placed in my body? I looked at Dr. Shukla, asking, "Are you sure that the circular nodule is a sarcoma?" Dr. Shukla compared my present CT scan on their computer, doing a measurement looking for a size comparison to determine if the nodule in my lung had grown. It appeared there was no growth. I looked at the ceiling whispering, "Thank you, dear Lord."

Dr. Stephans talked with us, and he showed us my CT scan which showed that the circular tissue was still shrink ing. He talked with us about the nodule in my lung, telling us it could be a small virus, as there is no visible growth now. I heard the greatest words I was hoping to hear. Smiling, Dr. Stephans told us, "Carl, we will see you in seven months." Boy, I felt great leaving the clinic's Oncology Department and now on our way to see D r. Sircharan Chalikonda.

Dr. Chalikonda and his RN, Nurse Lisa Taylor, entered the examination room, and once again I heard the doctor say, "Carl, the tissue on your bowel is still shrinking, and if it was a sarcoma, it would not shrink but grow. You made a good decision about waiting to see if it would grow when you were here three months ago."

I replied, "Does this mean I have graduated?" We were laughing as once again I looked up at the ceiling, whisper ing, "Thank you, dear Lord."

We are now back home, and today I have finished my story this September 22, 2012, where one year ago I was in surgery at the Cleveland Clinic to remove the Little Devil *who took my left kidney.* I thank Dr. Bipan Chand, his associate Dr. Kevin El - Hayek, Dr. Kevin Stephans, Dr. Sircharan Chalikonda, Dr. Charles, Dr. Gibson, and other associates for saving or prolonging my life. I thank each one for their instructions, which have helped me to recover in the clinic. *My advice to any person is always get a yearly physical. If you discover you have my disease, contact the Cleveland Clinic, fallow the doctor's instructions, and I hope your life will be saved or prolonged."*

Again, thank you to the doctors, nurses, their assistants, the technicians, and the staff, who continued to check on me and were always there to help me and my wife. Thank you to all the clinic employees who cleaned our room, removed the trash, and changed the linens on our beds. I am now in a recovery mode waiting for another CT scan at the Cleveland Clinic on March 29,2013. Yep, I am a human.

Today is March 29, 2013, and at 10:00 p.m., Sandra and I have returned home from the clinic where I had received my CT scan with the results explained by Dr. Kevin Stephans. No other Little Devil's friends were found. The tissue on my bowel was still shrinking and the small nodule in my right lung had not grown. So I am still in a recovery mode- thank you, God- and waiting for another CT scan at the Cleveland Clinic in seven months.

Another seven months has passed, and my wife and I are returning to the Cleveland Clinic for another CT scan to determine if the Little Devil or any of his friends are in my body. On October 29, 2013, at 6:00 am, we arrived at the clinic. My appointment wasn't until 11:30 a.m. You won't believe what you are going to read next.

I was asleep in bed about 2:45 a.m. when something was standing next to my bed with a pillow above my head, attempting to suffocate me. I believe that the Little Devil or his friends were trying to get even with me. I jumped out of our bed throwing my fists in the empty air when my wife hollered, "Honey, what are you doing?"

I replied, "Someone or something is trying to suffocate me with a pillow." I turned on the bedroom light to see my wife sitting up in bed with her hand over her eyes, attempting to shield the light, and shaking her head. I finally acknowledged to her after turning off the light and return ing to bed, "Honey, I believe I was dreaming," even though I was wondering if it was the Little Devil or his friends.

You know what it's like when you try to sleep and can't sleep? You roll around in bed changing positions, and finally I said, "Honey, are you having trouble sleeping? I cannot go to sleep."

She replied, "Yes, after you jumped out of bed." I suggested we get up, dress, and go to Cleveland now rather than wait for another three hours. So, at 3:30 a.m., we were on the road to the Cleveland Clinic. I had my CT scan with the help of the clinic's technician Joshua Carnes assisting me, and it was great to see him again. I then visited with Dr. Kevin Stephans at the clinic Oncology Department, who had reviewed my CT scan and showed it to us on his computer, telling us, "Carl, your circular tissue on your bowel is still shrinking, and the nodule in your right lung has not grown, so you are doing great. Keep doing what you have been doing, and we will see you for another CT scan in October 2014."

Boy, I have graduated to a year before another CT scan and once again I looked up at the ceiling thanking our dear Lord. While in the oncology clinic waiting room to receive my CT scan my wife and I had met another couple. The husband had my disease, which was another huge sarcoma that moved into his left leg muscle. I prayed for him. I had seen two other patients. A man was in a wheelchair being pushed by his wife, and another man had a tube protruding from this throat. I lowered my head praying for the two men.

Thank you, family and friends, for your prayers as I continue to recover from this disease.

ADDITIONAL INFORMATION

If you call the Cleveland Clinic, I used 1-800-223-2273 for a scheduled appointment after explaining about my liposarcoma. The operator transferred my call to Dr. Bipan Chand's office, where I was scheduled for an appointment. I was told they would send me in the mail my appointment confirmation, the directions to the clinic, and a map of the Cleveland Clinic campus. A great feature for people who have trouble walking, using a cane, or a wheelchair, there are clinic shuttle busses to transport you around their cam pus. There are so many friendly people wearing red jackets that will help you and direct you in and out of the clinic.

May our great and wonderful God bless you. Ask your family and friends for their prayers for you to our love and caring God during your struggle. I did, and I know it helped me. I hope my story will help you.

If you have any questions or want to contact me, you can reach me on the Internet at ckegerreis@yahoo.com.

- Carl Kegerreis

ABOUT THE AUTHOR

Picture of Carl Kegerreis reading his first published children's fiction book, Tibby and His Friend's Big Secret.

Carl Kegerreis is reading his first published children's book, *Tibby and His Friend's Big Secret*, a fiction book for children and animal lovers, published by Outskirts Press, January 2010. His second book, Fleeing a Country, Seeking a New Life, is a nonfiction book about a family fleeing a country and finding a new life in the US, published by the Bookstand Publishing Company, December 2011. Both books can be obtained on the Internet at Barnes & Noble, and Amazon (their kindle version), Outskirts

Press (their e-book), or other bookstores and retailers through their distributors, Ingram and Baker & Taylor. More information can be obtained on the Internet. Just Google, search Carl Kegerreis or his book titles.

Thank you for purchasing Who Is Going to Believe They Saved or Prolonged My Life? All royalties earned from this nonfiction book will be sent to the Cleveland Clinic for cancer research.

Carl Kegerreis attended Manchester College, Ball State University, and was drafted by the US Army his junior year. He spent three years in army security training and handling sentry dogs for the army's military Nike missile bases. He retired from the CSX Transportation Railroad 1999, work ing thirty-two years achieving Division Chief of Police. He lives in Ohio with his wife of fifty years, Sandra, with three children and five grandchildren.

www.ingramcontent.com/pod-product-compliance
Lightning Source LLC
Chambersburg PA
CBHW070333120526
44590CB00017B/2860